"We were a galaxy exploding into a million pieces, creating a whole new world, as we crashed against each other."
- Emme Rollins

Author: SOWEOPENONABOOK LTD
Graphic Designer: SOWEOPENONABOOK LTD

Copyright © 2021 by:
SOWEOPENONABOOK LTD

This Journal Belongs To:

My Socials

- :camera: Bookishthings173 ....
- :f: ....
- :tiktok: The-Bookworms ....
- **BB** ....
- :pinterest: ....
- :spotify: ....
- **g** ....
- **a** ....

My Yearly Reading Goals

200 audio

300 kindle

150 paperback

650 together

UPCOMING RELEASES I'M EXCITED ABOUT!

January

February

UPCOMING RELEASES I'M EXCITED ABOUT!

March

April

UPCOMING RELEASES I'M EXCITED ABOUT!

May

June

UPCOMING RELEASES I'M EXCITED ABOUT!

July

August

UPCOMING RELEASES
I'M EXCITED ABOUT!

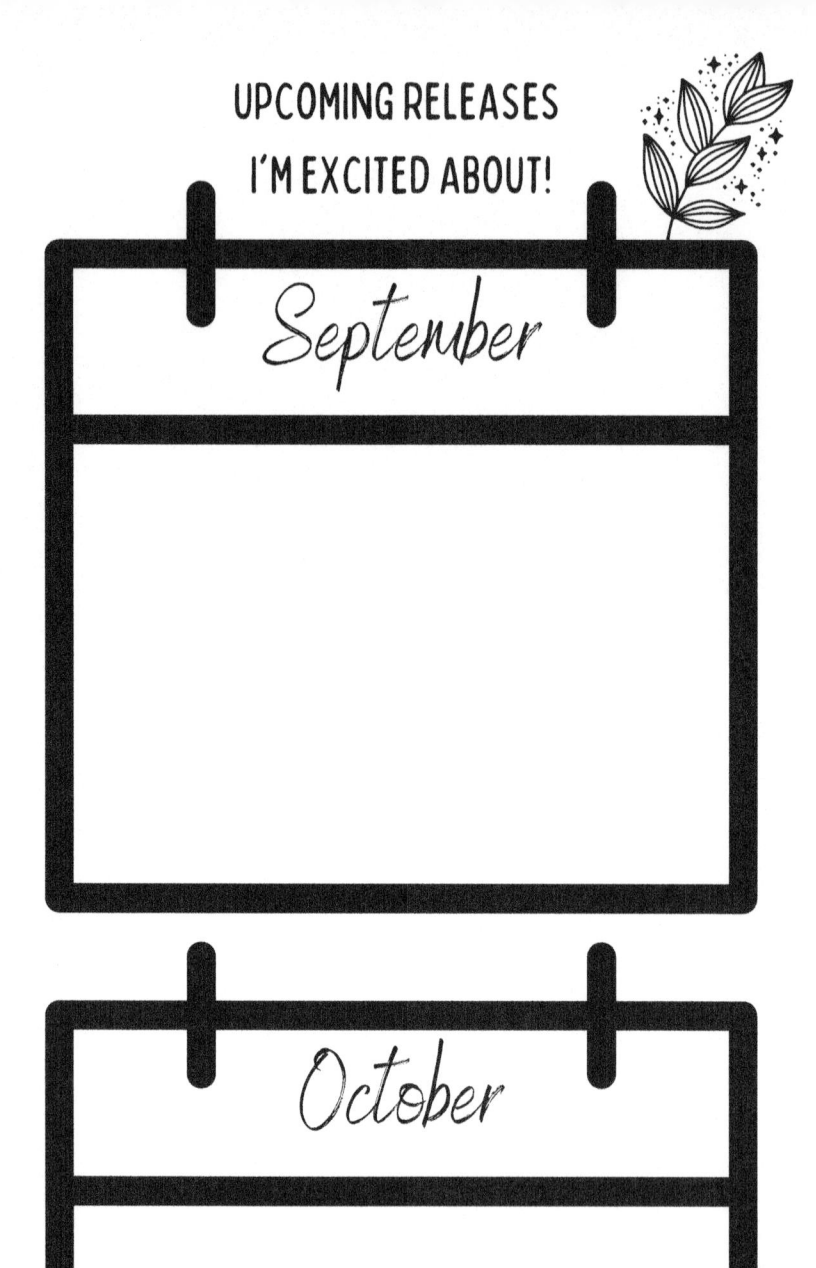

September

October

UPCOMING RELEASES I'M EXCITED ABOUT!

November

December

No8 zodiac academy

MY TBR

BOOK	AUTHOR	FINISH: Y/N?
Haunting Adeline	H D carlton	
Lady of rookgrave Manner	kathryn Moon	

MY TBR

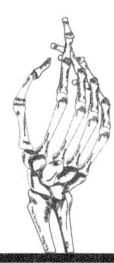

BOOK	AUTHOR	FINISH: Y/N?

MY TBR

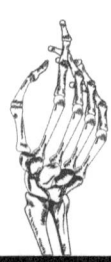

BOOK	AUTHOR	FINISH: Y/N?

MY TBR

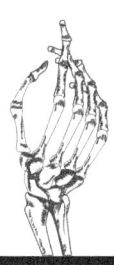

BOOK	AUTHOR	FINISH: Y/N?

MY TBR

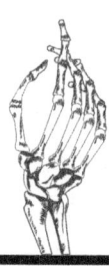

BOOK	AUTHOR	FINISH: Y/N?

LAPPING HER TONGUE ALONG MY NECK, SHE PULLS BACK, SEALING HER LIPS TO MINE IN A KISS THAT BRINGS ME TO THE BRINK OF SALVATION, *before stealing it away.*

-SAV R. MILLER

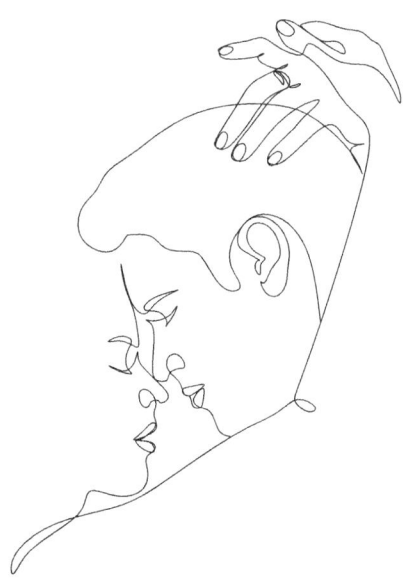

ARC TRACKER

BOOK/ AUTHOR	PR COMPANY	REVIEW DUE

ARC TRACKER

BOOK/ AUTHOR	PR COMPANY	REVIEW DUE

ARC TRACKER

BOOK/ AUTHOR	PR COMPANY	REVIEW DUE

ARC TRACKER

BOOK/ AUTHOR	PR COMPANY	REVIEW DUE

GET TO KNOW THE READER

FAVE PLACE TO READ:
Sofa, bed

AM/PM READING:
PM

FAVE SNACK WHILE READING:
Chocolate

HB/PB/EBOOK:
Any

FAVE GENRE: Romance / Fantasy

MY FAVE TROPES

Reveo Harem

ENL HEA

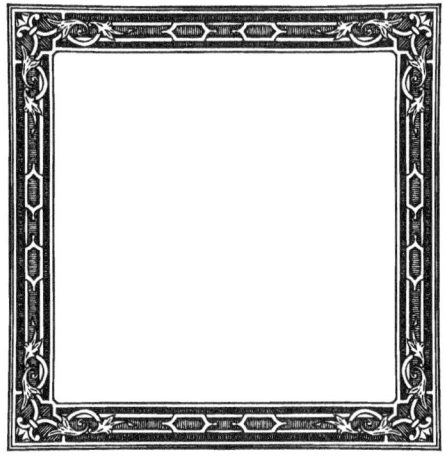

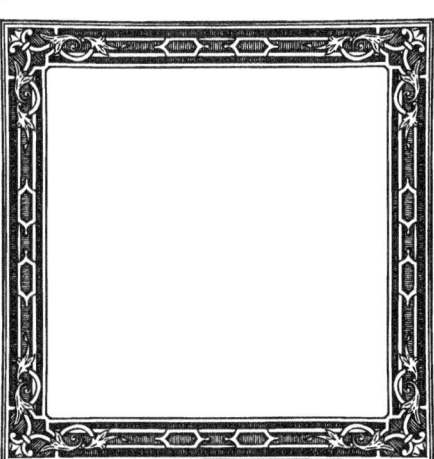

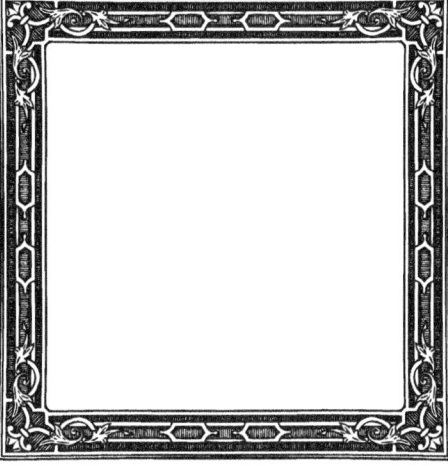

MY
FAVE TROPES

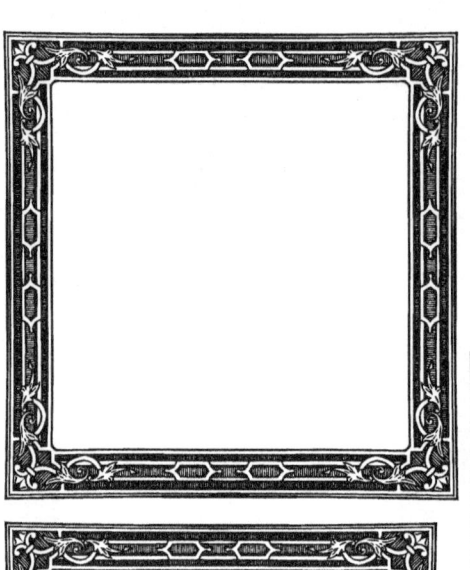

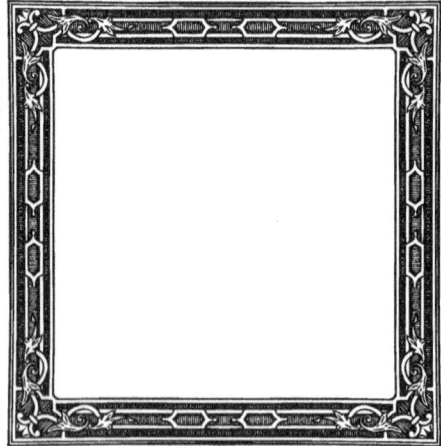
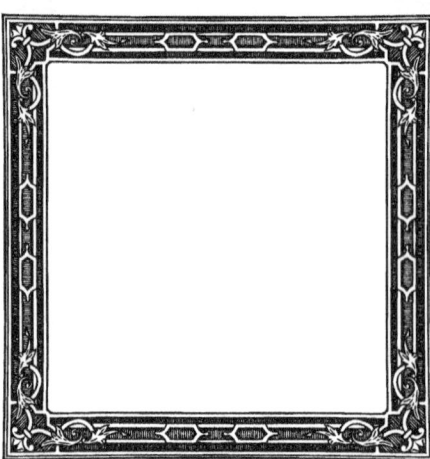
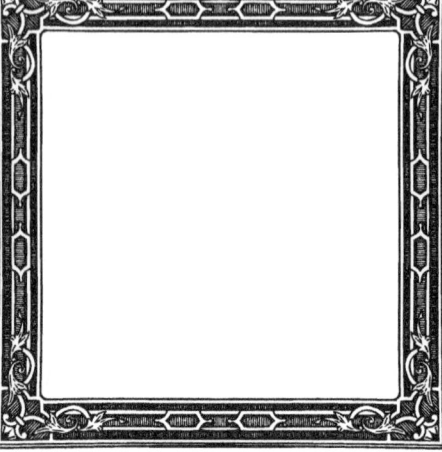

MY FAVE BOOKS

MY FAVE BOOKS

MY ONE-CLICK AUTHORS

- C M Stunich
- Britt Andrews

"He was a chaos of contradictions and I was a contradictory chaos."

—Giana Darling

MY FAVOURITE SPICY BOOKS I WILL ALWAYS RECOMMEND

MY FAVOURITE SPICY BOOKS I WILL ALWAYS RECOMMEND

- Havoc by C M Stunich
- Emrald Lake Britt Andrews

SMUT READERS DO IT BETTER

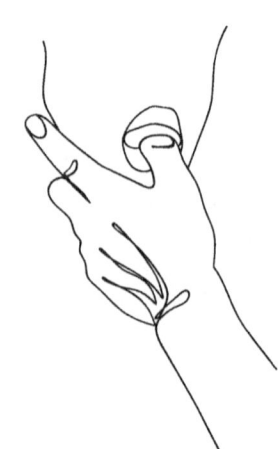

SCENES IN SPICY BOOKS THAT LIVE IN MY MIND RENT FREE

"I think Niko needs some help" Aren

Xavier raised his eyebrow "you want me to suck him off?"

Niko maybe a few bottom but he need relief too"

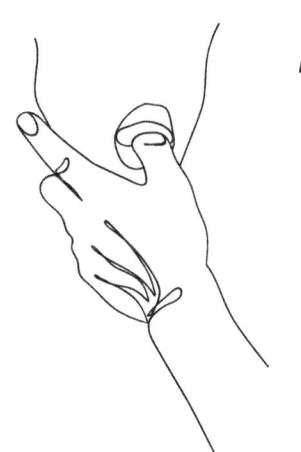

SCENES IN SPICY BOOKS THAT LIVE IN MY MIND RENT FREE

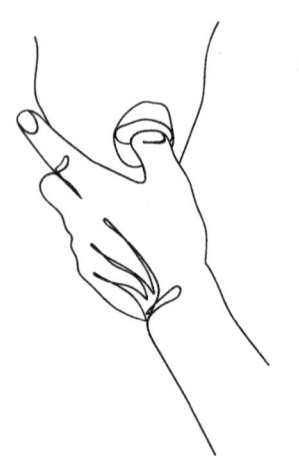

SCENES IN SPICY BOOKS THAT LIVE IN MY MIND RENT FREE

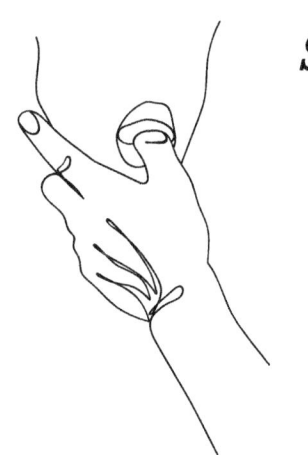

SCENES IN SPICY BOOKS THAT LIVE IN MY MIND RENT FREE

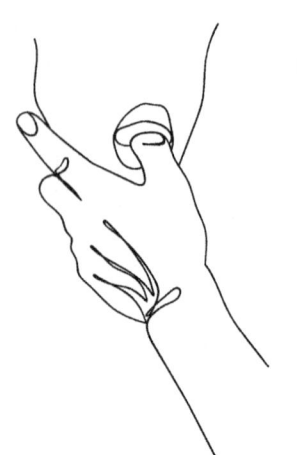

SCENES IN SPICY BOOKS THAT LIVE IN MY MIND RENT FREE

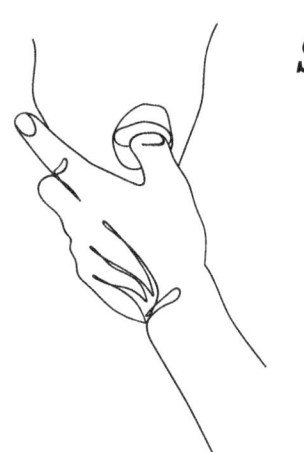

SCENES IN SPICY BOOKS THAT LIVE IN MY MIND RENT FREE

Tssssshh!!!

MY BOOK BOYFRIEND IS TALKING!

MY RIDE OR DIE
MALE CHARACTERS

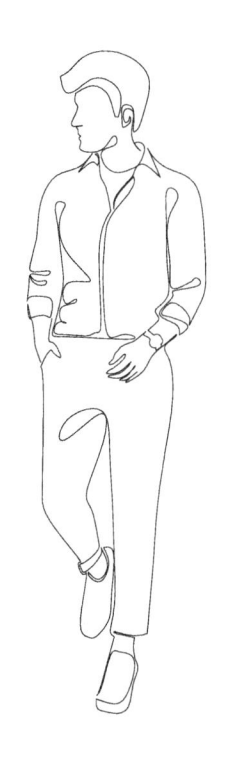

YEAH, MY BOYFRIEND'S PRETTY COOL BUT HE'S NOT AS *cool as me*

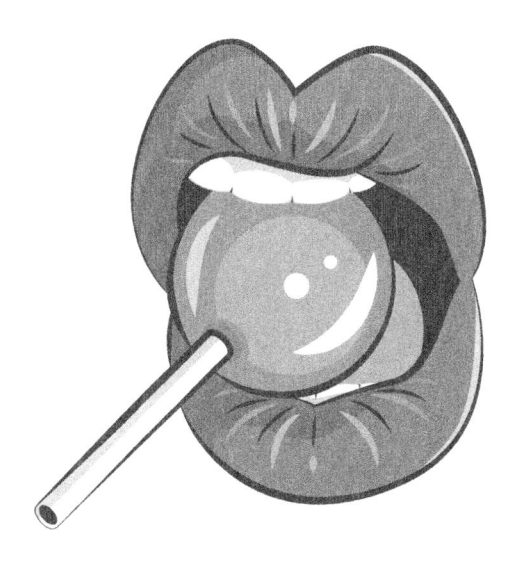

MY RIDE OR DIE
FEMALE CHARACTERS

"A MAN WHO STANDS IN FRONT OF A WOMAN DOES NOTHING MORE THAN BLOCK HER VIEW."

-PENELOPE DOUGLAS

MY RIDE OR DIE COUPLES

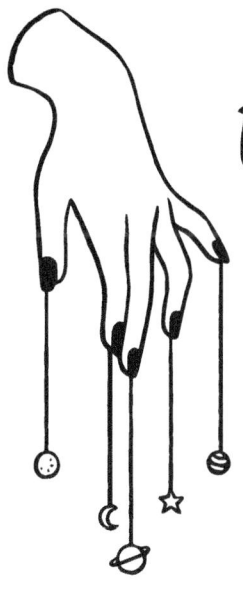

BUILD YOUR OWN FICTIONAL PERSON

(pick and choose features from your fave characters to build your perfect person!)

BUILD YOUR OWN FICTIONAL MAN

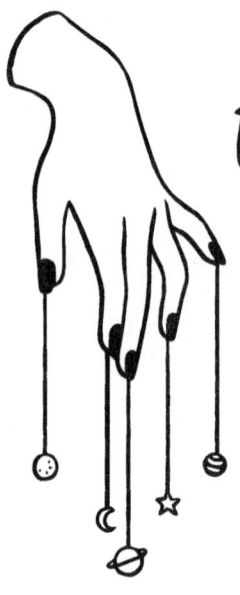

(pick and choose features from your fave male characters to build your perfect person!)

BUILD YOUR OWN FICTIONAL WOMAN

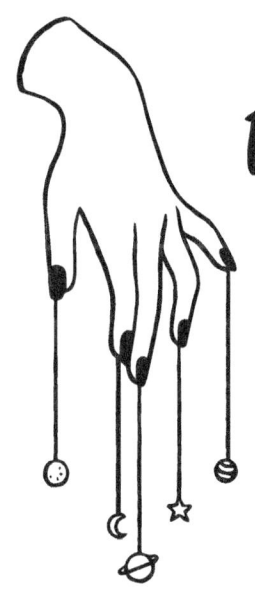

(pick and choose features from your fave female characters to build your perfect person!)

"DON'T YOU KNOW NOT TO RUN AWAY FROM PREDATORS, SWEETHEART?

We like the hunt."

—RUNYX

Yearly Mood Tracker

	J	F	M	A	M	J	J	A	S	O	N	D
1												
2												
3												
4												
5												
6												
7												
8												
9												
10												
11												
12												
13												
14												
15												
16												
17												
18												
19												
20												
21												
22												
23												
24												
25												
26												
27												
28												
29												
30												
31												

My Reviews

REVIEW SYSTEM

★☆☆☆☆ =

★★☆☆☆ =

★★★☆☆ =

★★★★☆ =

★★★★★ =

SPICE RATING

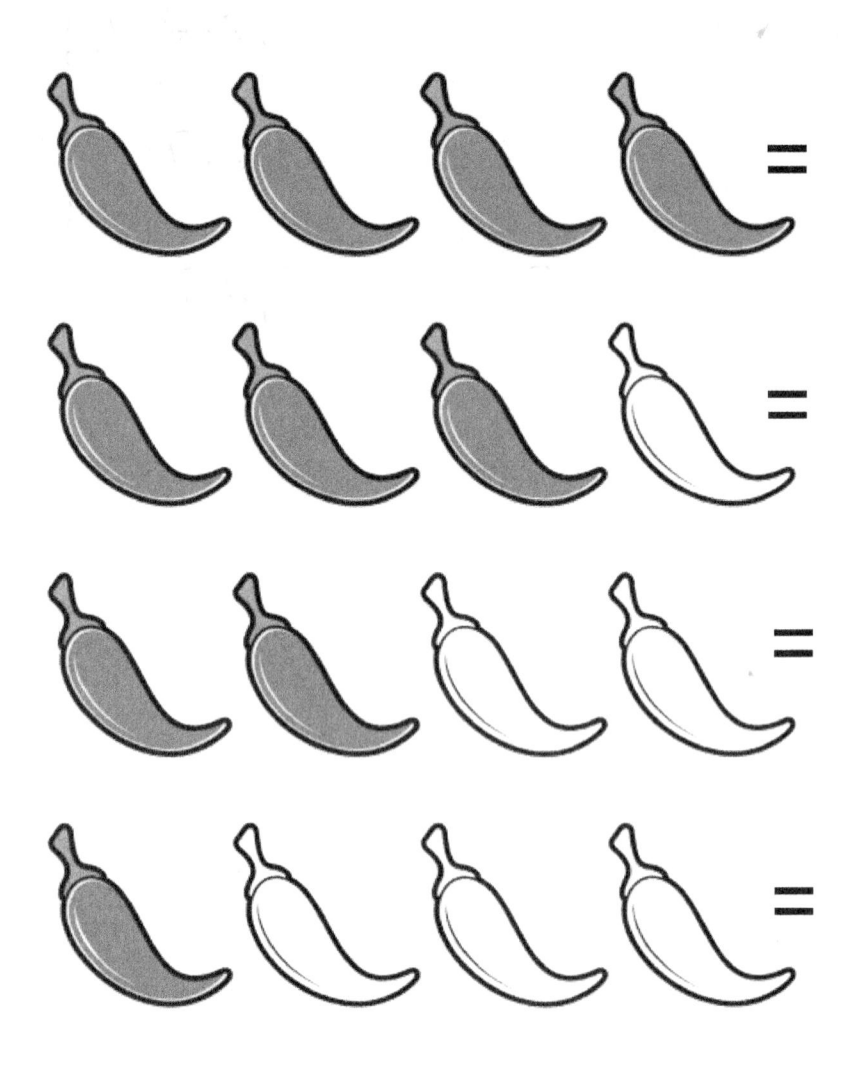

how spicy can you go?

Book Tracker

Author	Title	Genre	Rating
			☆☆☆☆☆
			☆☆☆☆☆
			☆☆☆☆☆
			☆☆☆☆☆
			☆☆☆☆☆
			☆☆☆☆☆
			☆☆☆☆☆
			☆☆☆☆☆
			☆☆☆☆☆

Book Tracker

Author	Title	Genre	Rating
Emma Dean	Spotted her first	~~Emma~~ RM/RMP	★★★★☆
Sam Hall	Pack heat	RH/PN	☆☆☆☆☆
	If the broom fits	RH/PN	☆☆☆☆☆
			☆☆☆☆☆
			☆☆☆☆☆
			☆☆☆☆☆
			☆☆☆☆☆
			☆☆☆☆☆
			☆☆☆☆☆

Book Tracker

Author	Title	Genre	Rating
			☆☆☆☆☆
			☆☆☆☆☆
			☆☆☆☆☆
			☆☆☆☆☆
			☆☆☆☆☆
			☆☆☆☆☆
			☆☆☆☆☆
			☆☆☆☆☆
			☆☆☆☆☆

Book Tracker

Author	Title	Genre	Rating
			☆☆☆☆☆
			☆☆☆☆☆
			☆☆☆☆☆
			☆☆☆☆☆
			☆☆☆☆☆
			☆☆☆☆☆
			☆☆☆☆☆
			☆☆☆☆☆
			☆☆☆☆☆

Book Tracker

Author	Title	Genre	Rating
			☆☆☆☆☆
			☆☆☆☆☆
			☆☆☆☆☆
			☆☆☆☆☆
			☆☆☆☆☆
			☆☆☆☆☆
			☆☆☆☆☆
			☆☆☆☆☆
			☆☆☆☆☆

Book Tracker

Author	Title	Genre	Rating
			☆☆☆☆☆
			☆☆☆☆☆
			☆☆☆☆☆
			☆☆☆☆☆
			☆☆☆☆☆
			☆☆☆☆☆
			☆☆☆☆☆
			☆☆☆☆☆
			☆☆☆☆☆

BOOK *Tracker*

	January	February	March	April	May	June	July	August	September	October	November	December
1												
2												
3												
4												
5												
6												
7												
8												
9												
10												
11												
12												
13												
14												
15												
16												
17												
18												
19												
20												
21												
22												
23												
24												
25												
26												
27												
28												
29												
30												
31												

Number of Pages

☐ 0-10

☐ 10-20

☐ 20-30

☐ 30-40

☐ 40+

BOOK *Tracker*

	January	February	March	April	May	June	July	August	September	October	November	December
1												
2												
3												
4												
5												
6												
7												
8												
9												
10												
11												
12												
13												
14												
15												
16												
17												
18												
19												
20												
21												
22												
23												
24												
25												
26												
27												
28												
29												
30												
31												

Number of Page

- 0-10
- 10-20
- 20-30
- 30-40
- 40+

"YOU WERE STILL MINE."

I CURLED MY HAND AROUND THE BACK OF HER NECK WHILE KEEPING MY THUMB ON HER LIP.

"MINE TO FIGHT WITH. MINE TO PROTECT. MINE TO FUCK."

MY VOICE DROPPED.

"Mine to love."

–ANA HUANG

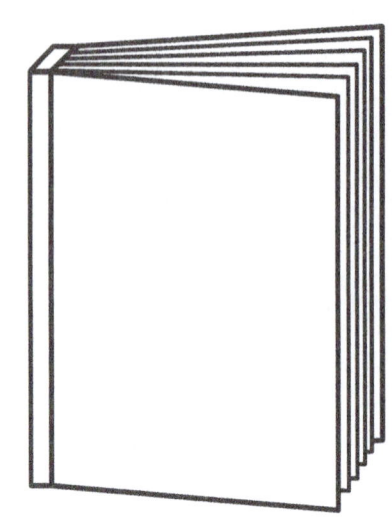

BOOK: Spotted her fire
AUTHOR: Emma Dean
TROPE: RH/paranormal
START: 30 Jan
FINISH:
PB/(EBOOK)/AUDIO:

MY RATING: ★★★★☆

SPICE RATING: 🌶🌶🌶🌶🌶

Pipers Mates are leppords and her blood can curse Rare Pack. but she is destand for much much more

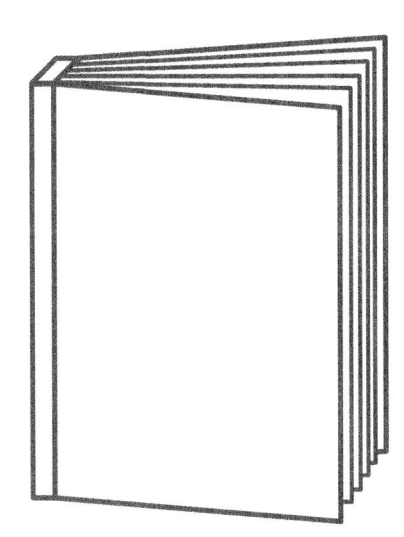

BOOK: Pack Loat
AUTHOR: SAM HALL
TROPE:
START:
FINISH:
PB/EBOOK/AUDIO: (EBOOK)

MY RATING: ★★★☆☆

SPICE RATING: 🌶🌶🌶🌶🌶

Not my favourite after a while But worth a reread later possibly. 3 Stars not enough

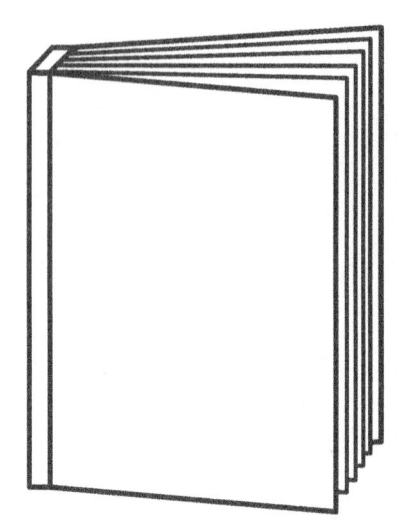

BOOK:
AUTHOR:
TROPE:
START:
FINISH:
PB/EBOOK/AUDIO:

MY RATING: ☆☆☆☆☆
SPICE RATING: 🌶🌶🌶🌶🌶

BOOK:
AUTHOR:
TROPE:
START:
FINISH:
PB/EBOOK/AUDIO:

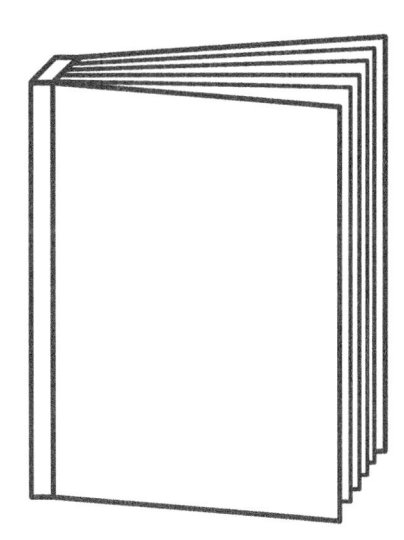

MY RATING: ☆☆☆☆☆
SPICE RATING: 🌶🌶🌶🌶🌶

BOOK:
AUTHOR:
TROPE:
START:
FINISH:
PB/EBOOK/AUDIO:

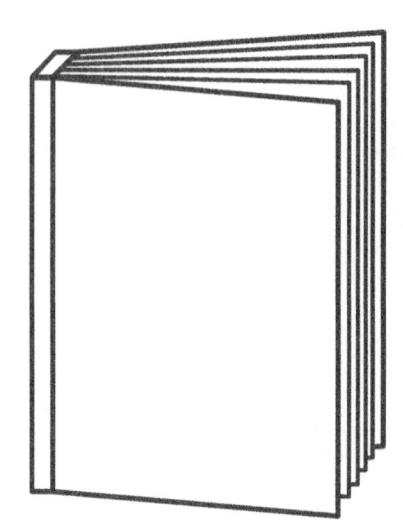

MY RATING: ☆☆☆☆☆
SPICE RATING: 🌶🌶🌶🌶🌶

BOOK:
AUTHOR:
TROPE:
START:
FINISH:
PB/EBOOK/AUDIO:

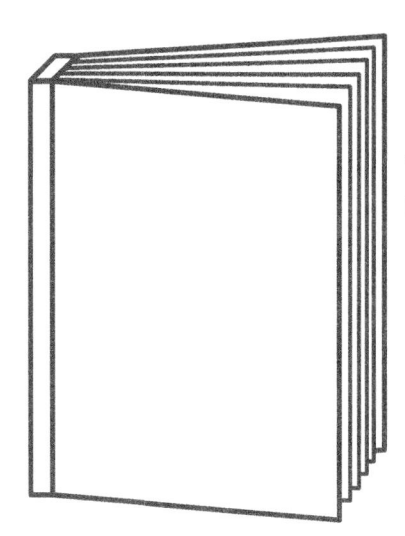

MY RATING: ☆☆☆☆☆
SPICE RATING: 🌶🌶🌶🌶🌶

BOOK:
AUTHOR:
TROPE:
START:
FINISH:
PB/EBOOK/AUDIO:

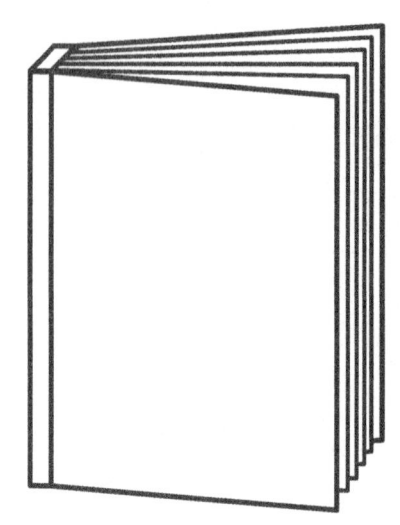

MY RATING: ☆☆☆☆☆
SPICE RATING: 🌶🌶🌶🌶🌶

BOOK:
AUTHOR:
TROPE:
START:
FINISH:
PB/EBOOK/AUDIO:

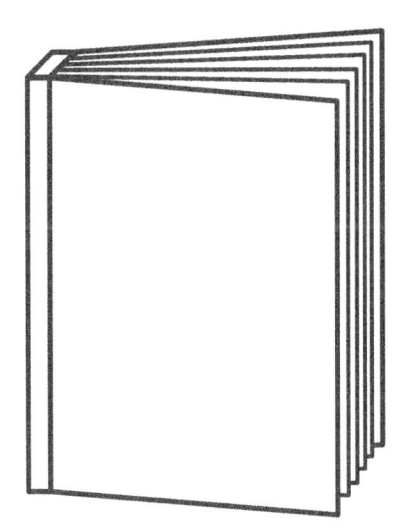

MY RATING: ☆☆☆☆☆
SPICE RATING:

BOOK:
AUTHOR:
TROPE:
START:
FINISH:
PB/EBOOK/AUDIO:

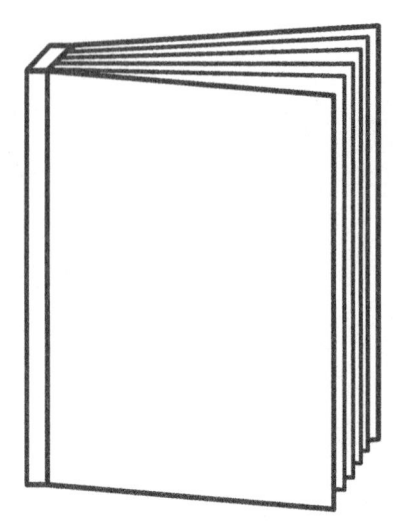

MY RATING: ☆☆☆☆☆
SPICE RATING: 🌶🌶🌶🌶🌶

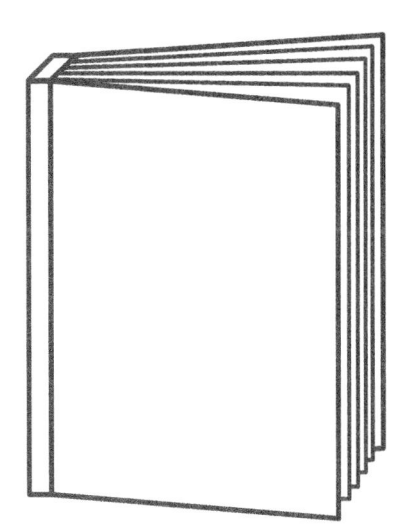

BOOK:

AUTHOR:

TROPE:

START:

FINISH:

PB/EBOOK/AUDIO:

MY RATING: ☆☆☆☆☆

SPICE RATING: 🌶🌶🌶🌶🌶

BOOK:
AUTHOR:
TROPE:
START:
FINISH:
PB/EBOOK/AUDIO:

MY RATING: ☆☆☆☆☆
SPICE RATING: 🌶🌶🌶🌶🌶

BOOK:
AUTHOR:
TROPE:
START:
FINISH:
PB/EBOOK/AUDIO:

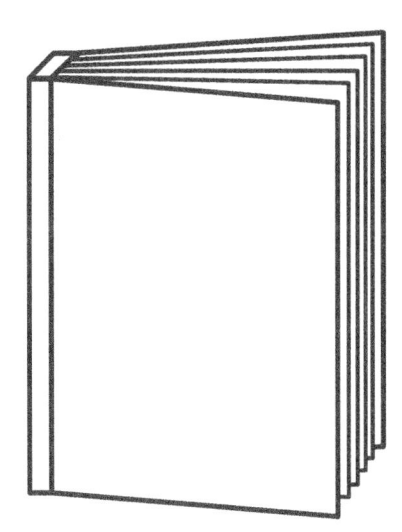

MY RATING: ☆☆☆☆☆
SPICE RATING: 🌶🌶🌶🌶🌶

BOOK:
AUTHOR:
TROPE:
START:
FINISH:
PB/EBOOK/AUDIO:

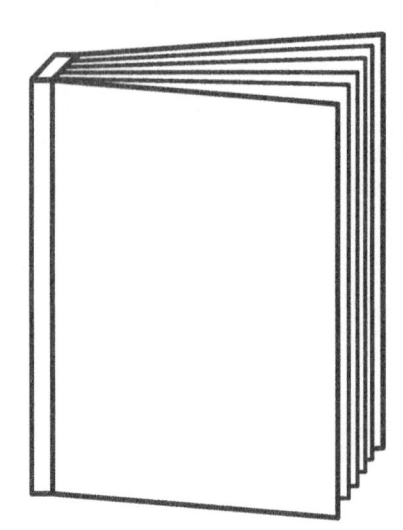

MY RATING: ☆☆☆☆☆
SPICE RATING: 🌶🌶🌶🌶🌶

BOOK:
AUTHOR:
TROPE:
START:
FINISH:
PB/EBOOK/AUDIO:

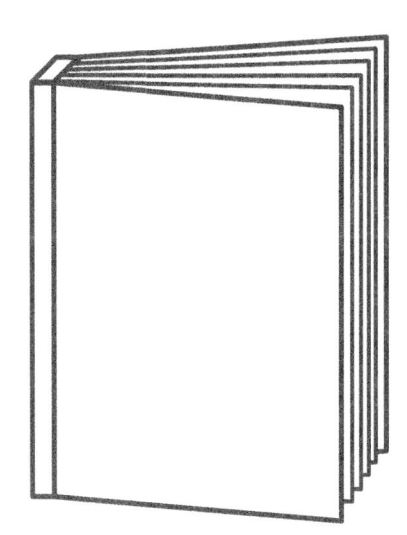

MY RATING: ☆☆☆☆☆
SPICE RATING: 🌶🌶🌶🌶🌶

BOOK:
AUTHOR:
TROPE:
START:
FINISH:
PB/EBOOK/AUDIO:

MY RATING: ☆☆☆☆☆

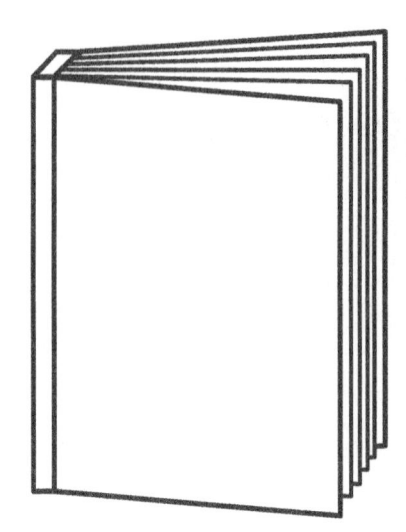

SPICE RATING:

BOOK:
AUTHOR:
TROPE:
START:
FINISH:
PB/EBOOK/AUDIO:

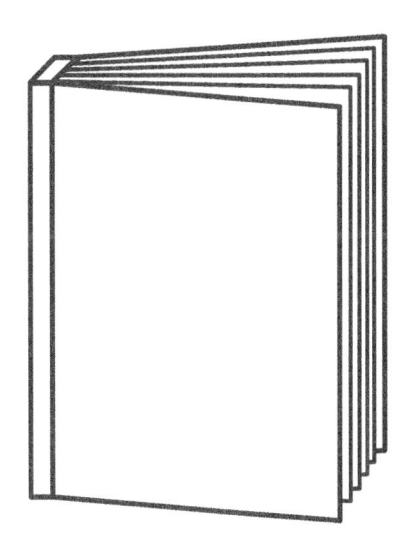

MY RATING: ☆☆☆☆☆
SPICE RATING: 🌶🌶🌶🌶🌶

BOOK:
AUTHOR:
TROPE:
START:
FINISH:
PB/EBOOK/AUDIO:

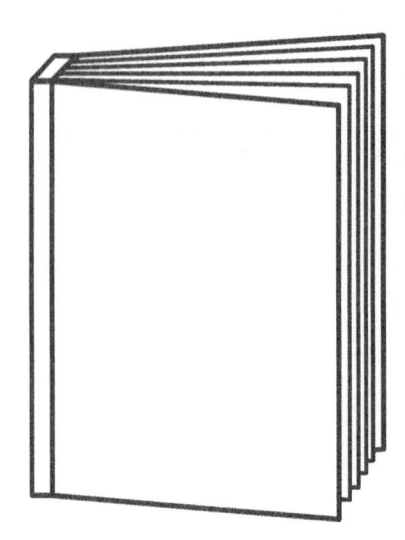

MY RATING: ☆☆☆☆☆
SPICE RATING: 🌶🌶🌶🌶🌶

BOOK:
AUTHOR:
TROPE:
START:
FINISH:
PB/EBOOK/AUDIO:

MY RATING: ☆☆☆☆☆

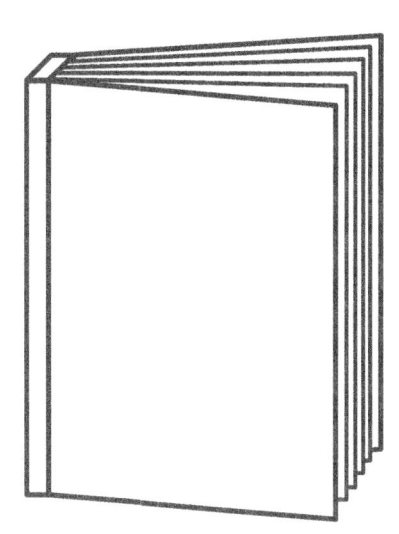

SPICE RATING: 🌶🌶🌶🌶🌶

BOOK:
AUTHOR:
TROPE:
START:
FINISH:
PB/EBOOK/AUDIO:

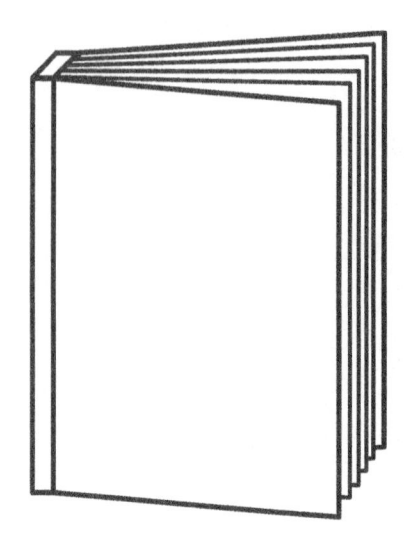

MY RATING: ☆☆☆☆☆
SPICE RATING: 🌶🌶🌶🌶🌶

BOOK:
AUTHOR:
TROPE:
START:
FINISH:
PB/EBOOK/AUDIO:

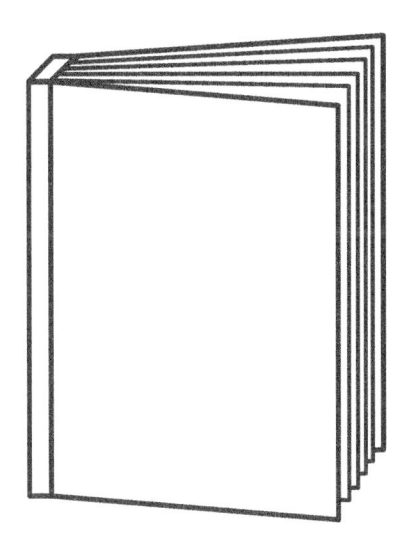

MY RATING: ☆☆☆☆☆
SPICE RATING: 🌶🌶🌶🌶🌶

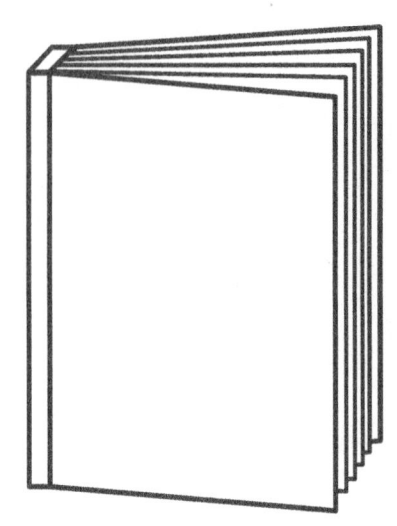

BOOK:
AUTHOR:
TROPE:
START:
FINISH:
PB/EBOOK/AUDIO:

MY RATING: ☆☆☆☆☆
SPICE RATING: 🌶🌶🌶🌶🌶

BOOK:
AUTHOR:
TROPE:
START:
FINISH:
PB/EBOOK/AUDIO:

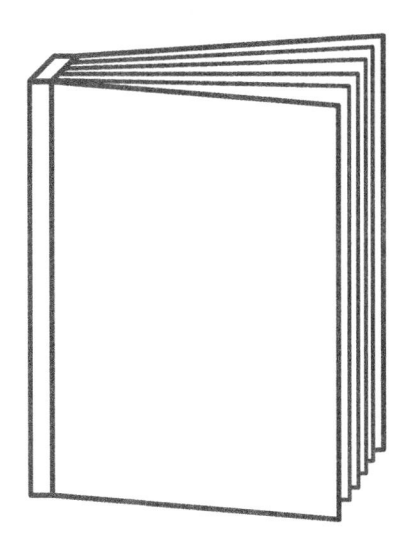

MY RATING: ☆☆☆☆☆
SPICE RATING: 🌶🌶🌶🌶🌶

BOOK:
AUTHOR:
TROPE:
START:
FINISH:
PB/EBOOK/AUDIO:

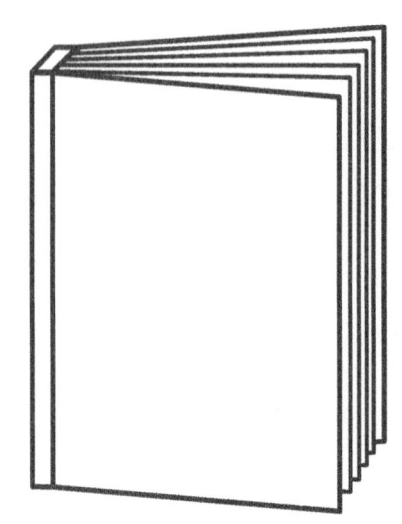

MY RATING: ☆☆☆☆☆
SPICE RATING: 🌶🌶🌶🌶🌶

BOOK:
AUTHOR:
TROPE:
START:
FINISH:
PB/EBOOK/AUDIO:

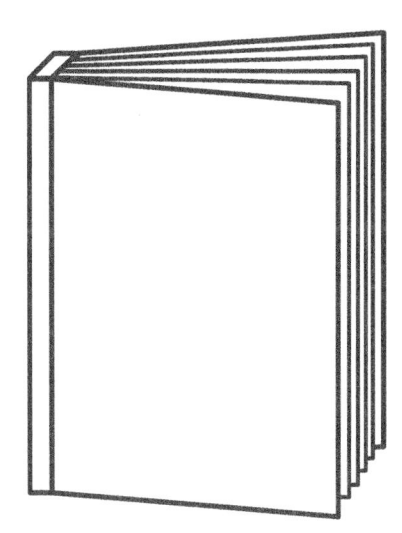

MY RATING: ☆☆☆☆☆
SPICE RATING: 🌶🌶🌶🌶🌶

BOOK:
AUTHOR:
TROPE:
START:
FINISH:
PB/EBOOK/AUDIO:

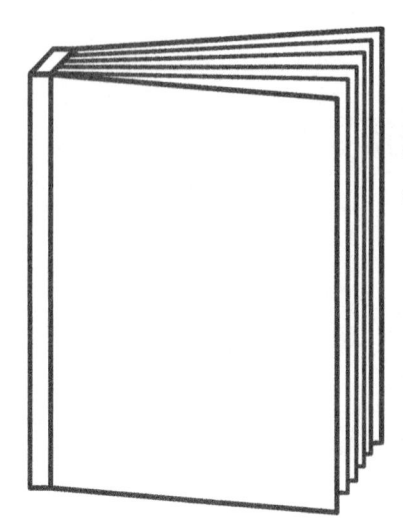

MY RATING: ☆☆☆☆☆
SPICE RATING: 🌶🌶🌶🌶🌶

BOOK:
AUTHOR:
TROPE:
START:
FINISH:
PB/EBOOK/AUDIO:

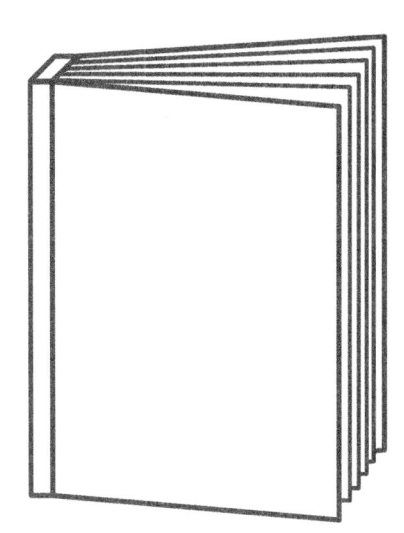

MY RATING: ☆☆☆☆☆
SPICE RATING: 🌶🌶🌶🌶🌶

BOOK:
AUTHOR:
TROPE:
START:
FINISH:
PB/EBOOK/AUDIO:

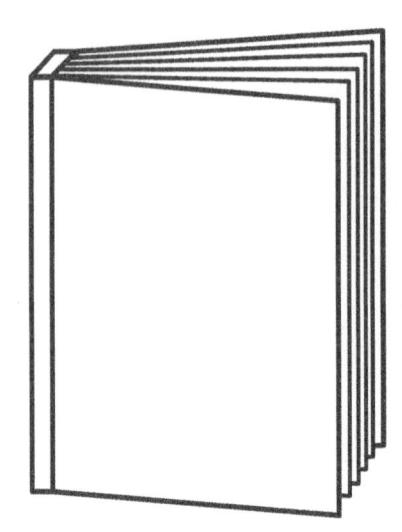

MY RATING: ☆☆☆☆☆
SPICE RATING: 🌶🌶🌶🌶🌶

BOOK:
AUTHOR:
TROPE:
START:
FINISH:
PB/EBOOK/AUDIO:

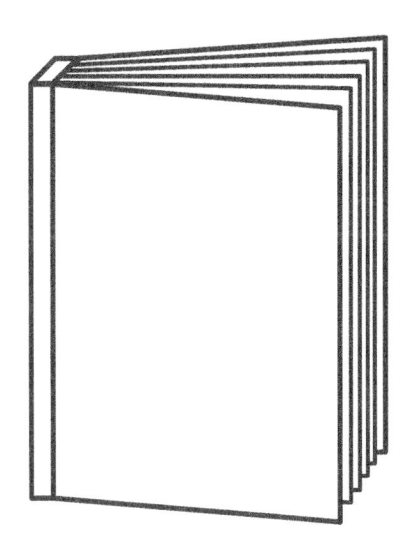

MY RATING: ☆☆☆☆☆
SPICE RATING: 🌶🌶🌶🌶🌶

HE LEANS OVER SO THE WARMTH OF HIS CHEST IS AN INCH AWAY FROM MY BACK AND HIS HOT BREATHS TICKLE THE SIDE OF MY FACE.

I'm going to fuck you and you're going to cry for me.

—RINA KENT

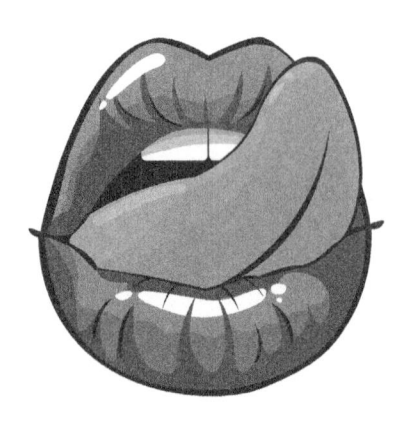

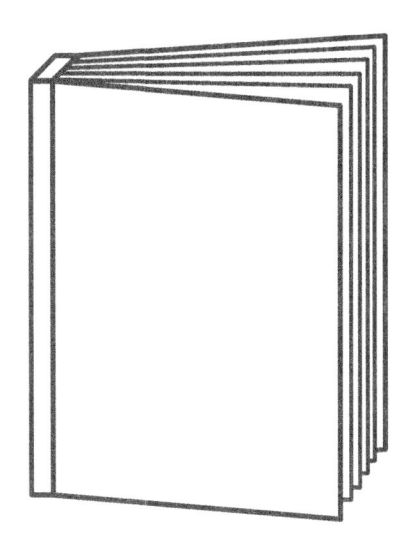

BOOK:
AUTHOR:
TROPE:
START:
FINISH:
PB/EBOOK/AUDIO:

MY RATING: ☆☆☆☆☆
SPICE RATING: 🌶🌶🌶🌶🌶

BOOK:
AUTHOR:
TROPE:
START:
FINISH:
PB/EBOOK/AUDIO:

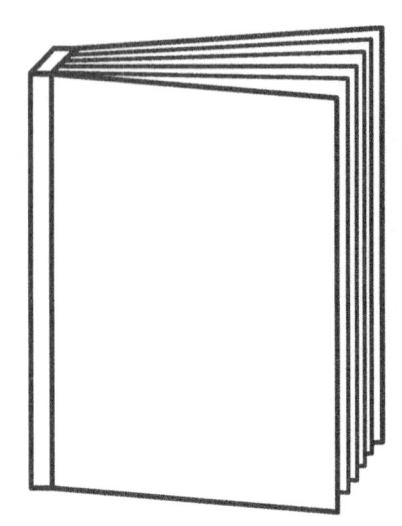

MY RATING: ☆☆☆☆☆
SPICE RATING:

BOOK:
AUTHOR:
TROPE:
START:
FINISH:
PB/EBOOK/AUDIO:

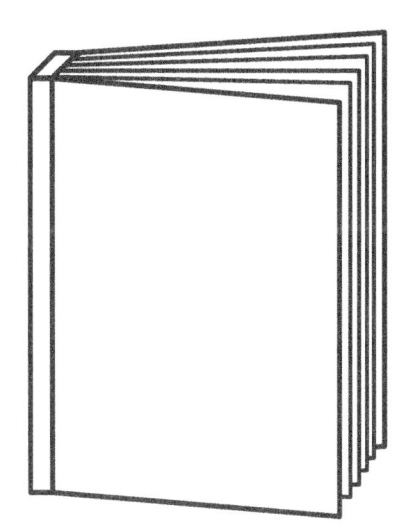

MY RATING: ☆☆☆☆☆
SPICE RATING: 🌶🌶🌶🌶🌶

BOOK:
AUTHOR:
TROPE:
START:
FINISH:
PB/EBOOK/AUDIO:

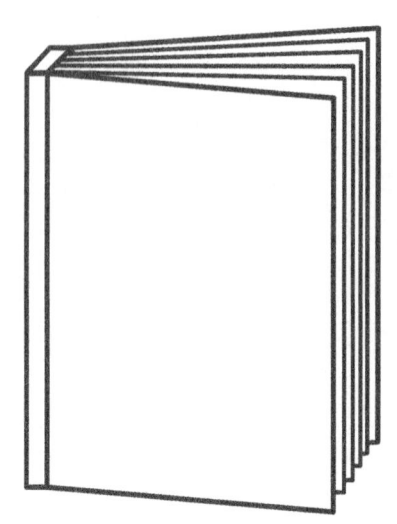

MY RATING: ☆☆☆☆☆
SPICE RATING:

BOOK:
AUTHOR:
TROPE:
START:
FINISH:
PB/EBOOK/AUDIO:

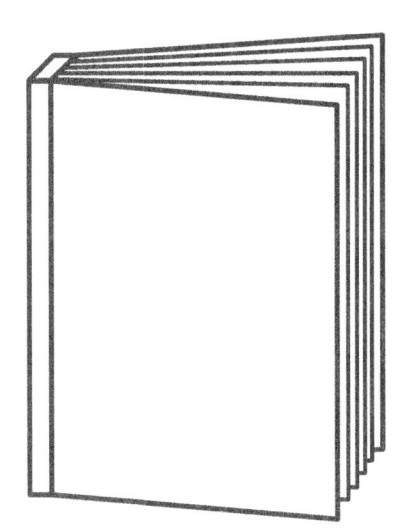

MY RATING: ☆☆☆☆☆
SPICE RATING: 🌶🌶🌶🌶🌶

BOOK:
AUTHOR:
TROPE:
START:
FINISH:
PB/EBOOK/AUDIO:

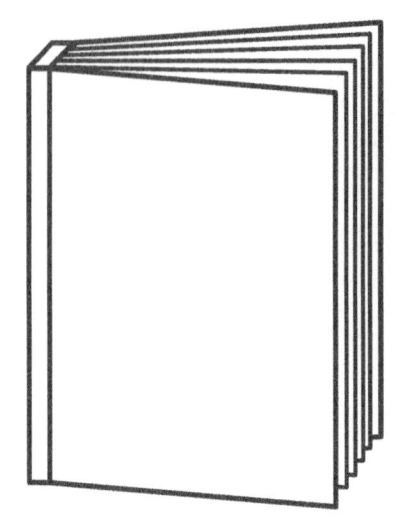

MY RATING: ☆☆☆☆☆
SPICE RATING: 🌶🌶🌶🌶🌶

BOOK:
AUTHOR:
TROPE:
START:
FINISH:
PB/EBOOK/AUDIO:

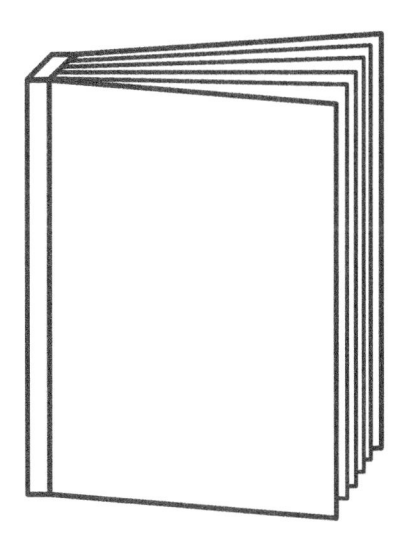

MY RATING: ☆☆☆☆☆
SPICE RATING: 🌶🌶🌶🌶🌶

BOOK:
AUTHOR:
TROPE:
START:
FINISH:
PB/EBOOK/AUDIO:

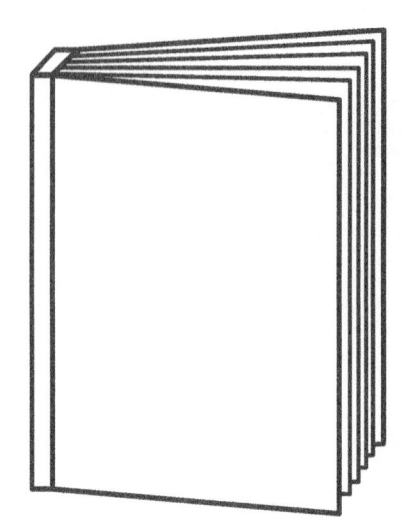

MY RATING: ☆☆☆☆☆
SPICE RATING: 🌶🌶🌶🌶🌶

BOOK:
AUTHOR:
TROPE:
START:
FINISH:
PB/EBOOK/AUDIO:

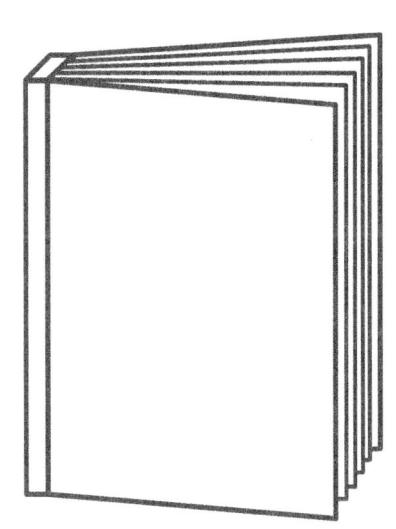

MY RATING: ☆☆☆☆☆
SPICE RATING: 🌶🌶🌶🌶🌶

BOOK:
AUTHOR:
TROPE:
START:
FINISH:
PB/EBOOK/AUDIO:

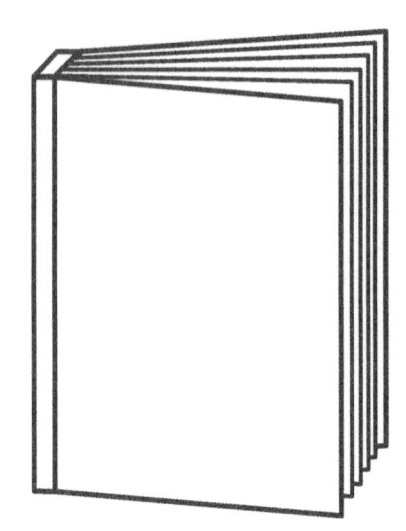

MY RATING: ☆☆☆☆☆
SPICE RATING: 🌶🌶🌶🌶🌶

"I WANT FREEDOM," SHE SAID FIERCELY.

"I GREW WINGS AFTER I LEFT YOU.
I SOARED WITHOUT YOU."

I'll burn your fucking wings.

—MIA KNIGHT

Monthly Reading Challenge

READ A BOOK STARTING WITH THE FIRST LETTER OF EACH MONTH!

Romance Reading Challenge

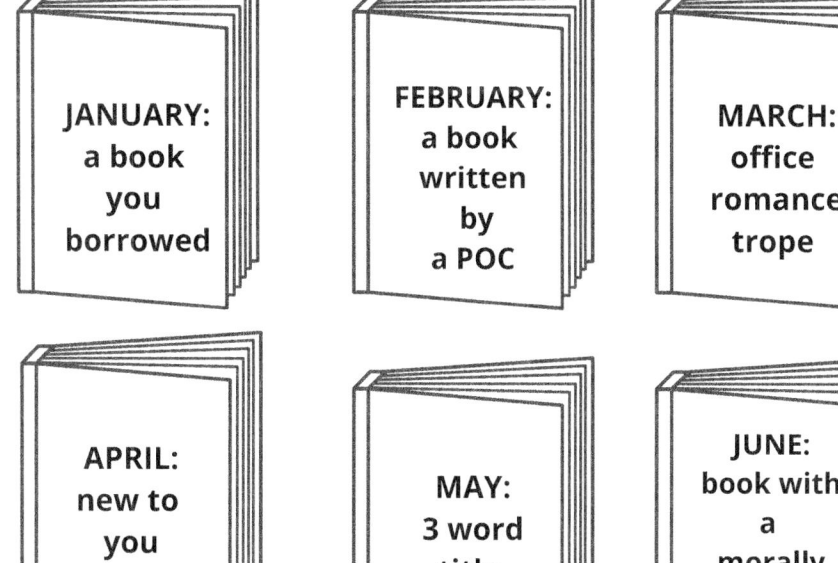

- **JANUARY:** a book you borrowed
- **FEBRUARY:** a book written by a POC
- **MARCH:** office romance trope
- **APRIL:** new to you author
- **MAY:** 3 word title book
- **JUNE:** book with a morally grey character
- **JULY:** book with summer vibes
- **AUGUST:** royal romance trope
- **SEPTEMBER:** sports romance trope
- **OCTOBER:** book with a spooky theme
- **NOVEMBER:** found family trope
- **DECEMBER:** christmas themed book

BOOKISH A-Z CHALLENGE!
READ A BOOK FOR EVERY LETTER!

A ....

B ....

C ....

D ....

E ....

F ....

G ....

H ....

I It ends with us - colleen hoover

J ....

K ....

L ....

M ....

N ....

O ....

P ....

Q ....

R ....

S
Spotted by her first - Emma Dean

T
The magic of eternity - Britt Andrews

U

V

W

X

Y

Z

I WANTED TO FU*K HER AND RUIN HER FOR ANYONE ELSE. I WANTED TO CRUSH HER WINGS AND THEN PUT THEM BACK TOGETHER AGAIN SO SHE'D BECOME DEPENDENT ON ME.

I wanted her to need me.

—DANIELLE LORI

Book Wish List

Title	Author	Price	Bought

Book Wish List

Title	Author	Price	Bought

Book Wish List

Title	Author	Price	Bought

Books Recommended By Friends

Books Recommended By Friends

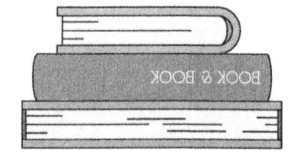

YOU'RE IN MY FUCKING BLOOD, AND I'LL TEAR APART ANYONE WHO DARES TO *Fucking Touch You.*

— SAFFRON A. KENT

BOOKS I OWN "TRACKER"

BOOKS I OWN "TRACKER"

BOOKS I OWN "TRACKER"

Spell Your Name In Books Challenge
(READ A BOOK STARTING WITH THE FIRST LETTER OF YOUR NAME)

L -
E -
I - It ends with us - colleen hoover
G -
H -

S - Spotted her frist Emma clean
M -
I -
T - The girl who loved Tom Gordon
H - hunger games

"A GIRL GETS CALLED A SLUT IF SHE HAS THE SEXUAL APPETITE OF A MAN. WELL, I'D WEAR THAT BADGE WITH PRIDE AND POLISH IT WITH MY *Middle Finger*"

−AMO JONES

SHELFIE

SHELFIE

SHELFIE

SHELFIE

BOOK QUOTES I LOVE

"If you dont come back for me. I'll come for you & It wont be pretty atlas corrigan"
"It wont be hard to find me"
"where everything B better"
"In boston" It ends with us C hoover

" BOOK QUOTES I LOVE

BOOK QUOTES I LOVE

"BOOK QUOTES I LOVE"

BOOK QUOTES I LOVE

BOOK QUOTES I LOVE

" BOOK QUOTES I LOVE

BOOK QUOTES I LOVE

BOOK QUOTES I LOVE

BOOK QUOTES I LOVE

"BOOK QUOTES I LOVE"

MY FAVOURITE BOOKS ON KINDLE UNLIMTED

KINDLE EMAIL:

MY FAVOURITE BOOKS ON KINDLE UNLIMTED

KINDLE EMAIL:

MY FAVOURITE BOOKS ON KINDLE UNLIMTED

KINDLE EMAIL:

MY FAVOURITE BOOKS ON KINDLE UNLIMTED

KINDLE EMAIL:

"I WANT TO FUCKING CONSUME HER. OWN EVERY FU*KING INCH OF HER, BODY AND SOUL UNTIL THE TRUTH IS BURNED INTO HER."

-VERONICA EDEN

BOOKS WITH THE BEST PLAYLISTS

....

....

....

....

....

....

....

....

BOOKS WITH THE BEST PLAYLISTS

....

....

....

....

....

....

....

....

SONGS THAT REMIND ME OF ...

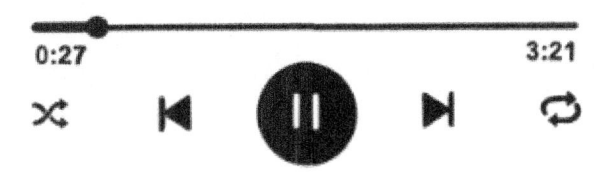

0:27 3:21

FAVE COUPLE

0:27 3:21

FAVE BOOK

SONGS THAT REMIND ME OF ...

0:27   3:21

FAVE SMUT SCENE

0:27   3:21

FAVE SAD SCENE

SONGS THAT REMIND ME OF ...

0:27 3:21

FAVE FEMALE CHARACTER

0:27 3:21

FAVE MALE CHARACTER

SONGS THAT REMIND ME OF ...

0:27   3:21

0:27   3:21

SONGS THAT REMIND ME OF...

0:27   3:21

0:27   3:21

SONGS THAT REMIND ME OF ...

0:27　　　　　　　　　　　3:21

0:27　　　　　　　　　　　3:21

I THINK YOU LIKE THE IDEA OF OTHER PEOPLE HEARING ME FUCK YOU UNTIL *your voice is hoarse.*

—LAUREN ASHER

FANTASY BOOKS I WANT TO READ

Sarah J Maas

High Mountain Court series
A. K. Mulford

> "FOR BLACK AND BROWN GIRLS, THE WORLD IS FULL OF SHARP EDGES, AND WITH EVERY STEP FORWARD, *we risk being cut.*"
>
> — KENNEDY RYAN

BOOKS BY POC AUTHORS I WANT TO READ

HE IS MY CAPTAIN.
AND FOR AS LONG AS
HE'LL HAVE ME,

I am his.

—GINA L. MAXWELL

LGBTQ BOOKS I WANT TO READ

SPOOKY BOOKS I WANT TO READ

MY FAVOURITE BOOKS WITH SPECIFIC KINKS

THEN I TASTE HIS LIPS AND HIS TONGUE, I BREATHE IN HIS SCENT, AND IT'S GASOLINE ON AN OPEN FLAME. I'M THE WOOD, HE'S THE ACCELERANT.

No matter how much we burn, we're never used up.

—SOPHIE LARK

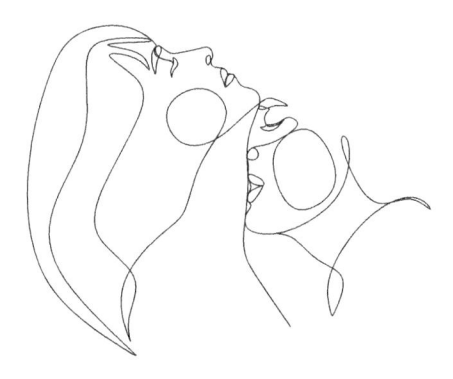

Reading Update

HOW MANY BOOKS DID YOU READ?

5	JANUARY
	FEBRUARY
	MARCH
	APRIL
	MAY
	JUNE
	JULY

Reading Update

HOW MANY BOOKS DID YOU READ?

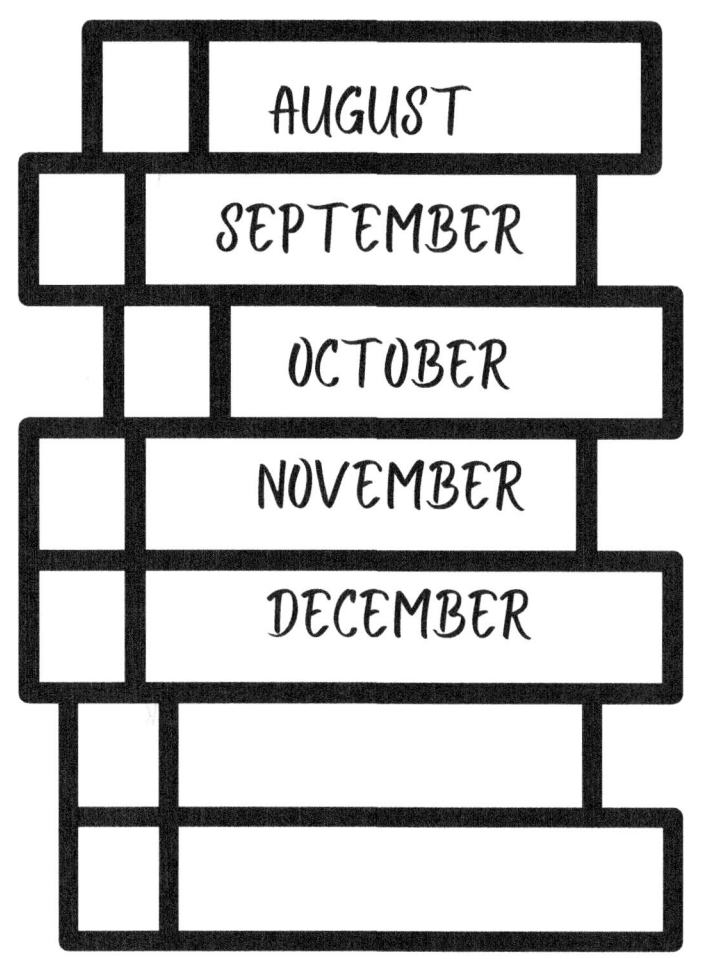

- AUGUST
- SEPTEMBER
- OCTOBER
- NOVEMBER
- DECEMBER

January SUMMARY

TOTAL NUMBER OF BOOKS READ?: 5

EBOOKS/KINDLE?: 3

PAPERBACKS? 1

AUDIOBOOKS? 1

NOTES

TOP FIVE BOOKS:

- The girl who loved fern garden
- It ends with us
- Emerald lake
- Sam Hall Book 1
- Sam Hall Book 2

February SUMMARY

TOTAL NUMBER OF BOOKS READ?:

TOP FIVE BOOKS:

EBOOKS/KINDLE?:

PAPERBACKS?

AUDIOBOOKS?

NOTES

March
SUMMARY

TOTAL NUMBER OF BOOKS READ?:

TOP FIVE BOOKS:

EBOOKS/KINDLE?:

PAPERBACKS?

AUDIOBOOKS?

NOTES

April
SUMMARY

TOTAL NUMBER OF BOOKS READ?:

TOP FIVE BOOKS:

EBOOKS/KINDLE?:

PAPERBACKS?

AUDIOBOOKS?

NOTES

May SUMMARY

TOTAL NUMBER OF BOOKS READ?:

TOP FIVE BOOKS:

EBOOKS/KINDLE?:

PAPERBACKS?

AUDIOBOOKS?

NOTES

June
SUMMARY

TOTAL NUMBER OF BOOKS READ?:

EBOOKS/KINDLE?:

PAPERBACKS?

AUDIOBOOKS?

NOTES

TOP FIVE BOOKS:

July
SUMMARY

TOTAL NUMBER OF BOOKS READ?:

TOP FIVE BOOKS:

EBOOKS/KINDLE?:

PAPERBACKS?

AUDIOBOOKS?

NOTES

August
SUMMARY

TOTAL NUMBER OF BOOKS READ?:

TOP FIVE BOOKS:

EBOOKS/KINDLE?:

PAPERBACKS?

AUDIOBOOKS?

NOTES

ts
September
SUMMARY

TOTAL NUMBER OF BOOKS READ?:

TOP FIVE BOOKS:

EBOOKS/KINDLE?:

PAPERBACKS?

AUDIOBOOKS?

NOTES

October
SUMMARY

TOTAL NUMBER OF BOOKS READ?:

EBOOKS/KINDLE?:

PAPERBACKS?

AUDIOBOOKS?

NOTES

TOP FIVE BOOKS:

November
SUMMARY

TOTAL NUMBER OF BOOKS READ?:

TOP FIVE BOOKS:

EBOOKS/KINDLE?:

PAPERBACKS?

AUDIOBOOKS?

NOTES

December
SUMMARY

TOTAL NUMBER OF BOOKS READ?:

EBOOKS/KINDLE?:

PAPERBACKS?

AUDIOBOOKS?

NOTES

TOP FIVE BOOKS:

"Don't move,"

HE ORDERED, AND SHE INSTANTLY STILLED.

"Good girl."

-SUZANNE WRIGHT

FAVE BOOKS

enter trope here

FAVE BOOKS

enter trope here

FAVE BOOKS

enter trope here

FAVE

enter trope here

BOOKS

FAVE BOOKS

enter trope here

HAPPY SCENES THAT LIVE IN MY MIND RENT FREE!

SAD SCENES THAT LIVE IN MY MIND RENT FREE!

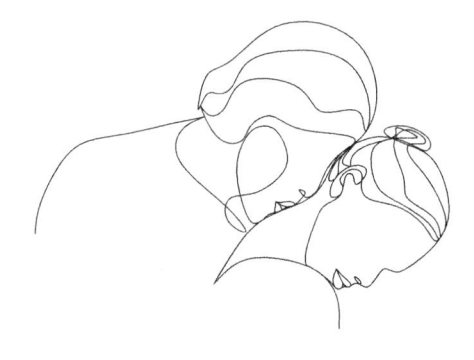

BEG ME FOR IT. ASK ME TO LET YOU COME,
and it's yours.

-R HOLMES

MY YEARLY ROUND-UP

NUM OF BOOKS READ

NEW AUTHORS I DISCOVERED

MY YEARLY ROUND-UP

FAVE QUOTE OF THE YEAR

FAVE BOOK OF THE YEAR

MY YEARLY ROUND-UP

BEST TROPE YOU READ

BEST GENRE YOU READ

MY YEARLY ROUND-UP

(ADD YOUR OWN)

MY YEARLY ROUND-UP

(ADD YOUR OWN)

"YOU DESERVE THE WORLD.
I'D BURN IT DOWN BEFORE I LET ANYONE *give you less.*"

-KV ROSE

EXTRA NOTES

EXTRA NOTES

EXTRA NOTES

"Kiss me."

"YOU'RE A FUCKING NIGHTMARE."

"Kiss me."

"YOU'RE RUINING MY LIFE."

"Kiss me."

—PEPPER WINTERS

Dump Page

Dump Page

Embrace the smut & spice

Printed in Great Britain
by Amazon